How to Prepare and Survive in a Foreign Country

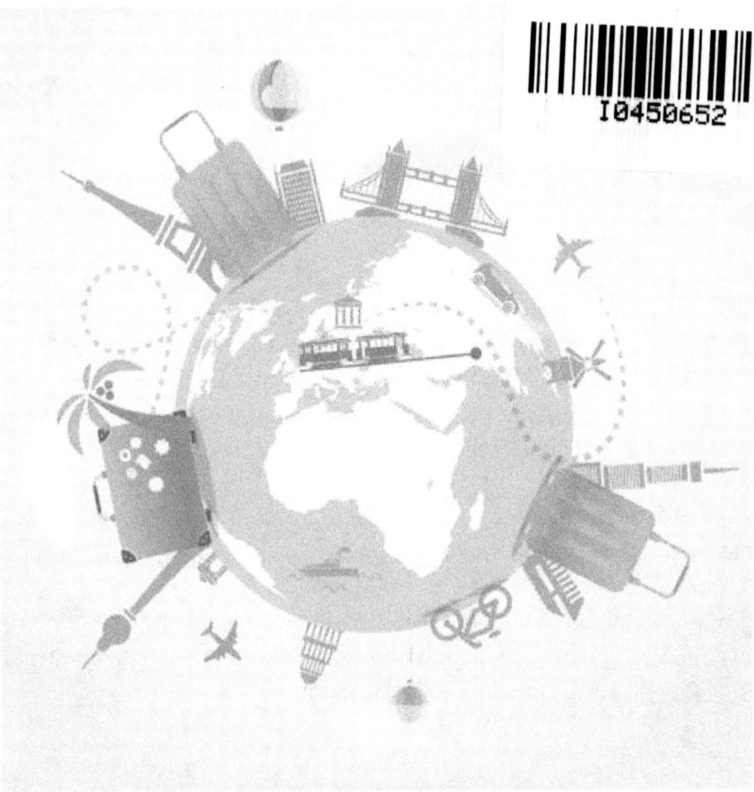

Colvin Tonya Nyakundi

Prepping and Survival Series

JD-Biz Publishing

Check out some of the other Entrepreneur Series books
Entrepreneur Series books on Amazon
Check out some of the Science of Living Series books
Science of Living Series on Amazon
Check out some of the Health Learning Series books
Health Learning Series on Amazon

Table of Contents

Introduction

People living in foreign countries can easily tell you that they encounter so many challenges in their day to day activities. Those living away from home for the first time normally feel loneliness and homesickness just a few weeks after moving into the foreign country. Others feel depressed and remain locked indoors for several weeks as they try to figure out how to adjust to the new environment.

With all these and many more challenges, all those planning to move into another country must thoroughly prepare for the kind of lifestyle waiting for them. With inadequate preparation, life could become very uncomfortable and therefore force them to come back home without achieving their goals. However, no need to worry about anything as life in another country could be so much interesting if you properly prepare and know how to adjust to different conditions.

Each year there are tens of millions of people around the world who migrate from one country to another or from one continent to another. Some prefer moving to neighboring countries while there are those who want to explore other parts of the world far, far away from home. Since most of them manage to adapt to the living conditions in their new countries, you can also manage to do it if you're willing to do everything possible to live there.

The book "How to Prepare and Survive in a Foreign Country" is equipped with everything that should be done by those planning to move abroad. After reading the book, you'll have ideas on how to prepare before moving abroad, what to do and what not to do when abroad. You'll also get to know how you can adjust your lifestyle to fit in the new country and cope with the numerous challenges facing foreigners in that country.

Investing back home or in the foreign country will be much easier as you'll know how to go about it after reading this book. Start your journey to a comfortable and fulfilling lifestyle abroad by reading "How to Prepare and Survive in a Foreign Country.

What to Consider When Moving Abroad

Making a decision to move abroad is not something that you can hurriedly do and then embark on the journey the following day. If you make such a mistake, you can end up encountering endless problems and setbacks in the foreign country with absolutely no ideas about what to do. Before you embark on a journey abroad, it is important that you take as much time as possible to consult widely before making the final decision. You must also consider the pros and cons of your trip and stay there. It is also of utmost importance that you list down all the objectives that you want to achieve and try to figure out whether you have the capacity to achieve them. Here are some of the things that you have to consider before moving abroad:

- Why are you planning to move to that country?

The reason as to why you want to move abroad will significantly affect how you're going to prepare and what or who you'll bring along or leave behind. If you are seeking asylum in another country after being exiled back home, you probably don't have many choices. You have to move out as quickly as possible into any country that accepts your plea.

On the other hand, if you're moving into another country as a tourist (for pleasure), you'll have plenty of time to prepare and pack everything. You have to do some research about the foreign country and book a hotel room where you'll be staying. You also have to identify a tour guide and fun-full activities to engage in while there. Since most tourists stay in foreign countries for just a few days or weeks, you probably don't need so many personal effects or huge sums of money.

There are several things that you should do if you're planning to move abroad for education purposes. Unless you're on a fully paid scholarship, you must have the money required to pay your tuition, accommodation, transportation, meals and other personal expenses. It is also important that you set aside some emergency cash as you never know what is going to happen.

You need to prepare how to live away for a long period of time if you're planning to work in a foreign country. Other reasons as to why people move abroad include seeking investment opportunities, induction courses, sports events and participation in a charitable course.

- How long are you planning to stay there

The length of your stay in a foreign country will be mostly determined by what you'll be doing there. Either way, this is what will determine the amount of money you'll need and what you'll have to carry. The nature of accommodation that you'll need will also be influenced by this factor. When planning to stay abroad for prolonged periods, you'll have to make arrangements for more permanent accommodation such as an apartment or condo. Due to the fact that hotel rooms are quite expensive, they are only suitable for those planning to stay there for a short period of time.

- How is the weather/climate in that country?

During winters in some countries in the northern hemisphere (e.g. Iceland) you can stay for several weeks without seeing the sun for even a second. During this period, the temperature is freezing and there is very little activity you can engage in while there. On the other hand, some countries experience excessively hot temperatures during certain times of the year. In some Asian countries such as Saudi Arabia and the United Arab Emirates, several people have collapsed and died as a result of the extremely hot temperatures during certain seasons of the year. In Australia, bush/forest fires are quite common during certain times of the year and they always result in several deaths for those caught unawares. You must therefore consider the weather and/or climate conditions in a foreign country before making a decision to move there during certain times of the year. If you decide to move to any country, you must be prepared for any weather extremity that may be experienced while you're there.

- How is lifestyle there?

If you're keen on enjoying your stay in a foreign country you have to consider the kind of lifestyle there. For instance, if you are addicted to the internet you have to consider its penetration in that country. If the average internet connectivity speed is quite low or unavailable in most parts, you have to think of doing something else during your free time. Other things to consider include availability and accessibility to entertainment joints such as theatres, football stadiums or tennis courts, night clubs and casinos.

- Do you have a family?

Are you a family man or woman? The amount of time that you'll be spending abroad will determine whether you're going to bring your children along or leave them behind. If you're moving abroad for a short period of time and decide to leave your kids back home, you have to make arrangements about where you're going to leave them. If you decide to bring them along since you'll be staying in your new country for a very long period of time you have to make sure that their education is not affected in anyway. This means that you have to find a school offering the same curriculum as your home country. The school must also have several other students from your home country so that you kid(s) doesn't feel lonely or the odd one out. The size of your family will also determine the type, location and size of required accommodation. Those with school going children have to live near a library or the school.

- How will the local political conditions affect your stay there?

If you're moving- maybe to work -in a country experiencing civil war, you must always be prepared for frequent and sporadic gunfire at any time of the day. This means that you should avoid the insecure areas/regions as much as possible and only go there if it is absolutely necessary. If possible, you can seek protection from the local government or the United Nations while working in such a country. Some countries experience a period of instability, unrest and violence during electioneering seasons. You should therefore avoid such countries during these seasons or ensure that you don't visit unsafe areas.

- What is the cost of living?

According to statistics from research carried out by reputable firms, some of the most expensive cities in the world include Tokyo, Singapore, Paris, Geneva, Melbourne, Oslo and Caracas. If you are coming from a region where the cost of living is quite cheap, you have to be fully prepared for the high cost of living in cities such as the ones listed above. Before moving to any country/city, it is important that you do some research on the average cost of living there so that you can set aside enough money to help you stay there comfortably. If you are going to work in a foreign country, it's important that you make sure that you'll be earning enough money to sustain your stay there and still save some money for investments back home or there.

- How many people from your home country currently live there?

The higher the number of people from your country, the more you're likely to enjoy your stay in a foreign country. You can organize events targeting people from your home country so that you don't feel bored or lonely. A high number of people from your home country indicate that they like staying there and hence you're also likely to enjoy your stay there. In case you encounter some problems or challenges while abroad, you're likely to get more help from your fellow countrymen and women than from any other person.

How to Save Money While Abroad

Regardless of the reasons as to why people move abroad, it is everybody's wish to save as much money as possible during their stay in another country. Unless you know how to save money while there, you can easily come back home poorer than you left. However, if you adequately prepare before moving abroad and then work hard towards achieving your goal, you'll definitely come back home richer and more financially stable. If you're keen on saving some money while staying abroad, then you have to consider the following points:

- Consider purchasing or renting a condo/apartment instead of living in a hotel room

The cost of renting a hotel room for several months is quite high when compared to renting or purchasing a hotel room. The best thing to do when planning to stay abroad for several months is rent a fully furnished condo or apartment. If you'll be staying there for several years you'll probably need to purchase the condo or apartment as it will be even cheaper. Remember that you can still re-sell the apartment once you're ready to move back home.

The United Nations and other International Organizations provide accommodation for some or all their employees working away from their home countries. If you'll be working under such organizations, you need to check with your superiors so as to establish if they can make arrangements for your accommodation. This way you'll get to save the money that you could have used in hotel rooms or to purchase or rent an apartment.

When going to another country for studies, you need to check if your institution can provide you with accommodation. If you're on scholarship requesting your financier to pay your accommodation is one way of saving some money.

- Consider working if you're a student

Some countries such as the United Kingdom allow foreign students to work near their schools during their free time. You can therefore save some money by earning some extra cash during your stay in such countries.

- Consider using public means of transportation to and from work

Unlike private cars and cabs, public means of transportation such as trains and busses are quite cheap in any country. You can therefore save a lot of money by simply using this means of transportation unless you don't have an alternative. Even when touring popular attractions or different towns within the foreign country, it is still advisable that you use public means of transportation.

You need to enroll to a local driving school if you prefer using private means of transportation but motorists drive on the opposite side of the road. Remember that driving yourself is much cheaper and convenient than hiring a permanent driver.

- Group tours

Rather than touring a given country or town as an individual or with your family, you can save some money by touring as a group. Transportation will be much cheaper and most hotels give discounts to those booking several rooms at the same time.

- Avoid unnecessary expenditure such as impulse buying

One of the easiest ways of wasting money is buying something because you like but don't need it or simply because you've seen somebody else purchase it. You can save some money while abroad if you avoid spending your money on unnecessary things. Budgeting how you'll spend your money during a given month and sticking to the budget is the surest way of avoiding impulse buying.

- Use diplomatic channels when importing commodities

Some countries exempt the United Nations, charitable organizations and foreign missions from regular importation and other types of taxes. You can therefore save some money by importing commodities through your organization rather than importing them as an individual.

How to Relate With Locals in a Foreign Country

Moving into another country is one of those life decisions that need careful consideration and accurate analysis. The situation is even more challenging if you don't have a relative or friend there to receive you and guide you during the first few days of your stay. Regardless of how long you'll be staying there or what you'll be doing, one thing that you can't avoid is relating or interacting with the locals. This means that you might as well prepare how you are going to interact or relate with them. These are some of the things that you should or shouldn't do so as to enjoy your stay abroad:

- Participate in communal events

One way of showing that you care about the local community is participation in local social events. You can show up whenever there is a community gathering to solve a common problem or during events such as tournaments. By simply showing up at such events, you'll get to interact and know more people and hence you'll increase the number of friends in that country.

- Help out whenever you can

Whenever you're in a position to help one of the locals seeking your help, you should do so without having second thoughts. You'll be better off when somebody owes you than when you owe somebody a favor. You will also get to create many friends who will come in handy when you need something in future.

- Blend in with the local community

Blending in with the local community basically means embracing their culture, traditions and lifestyle instead of trying to stick to your own norms. Most locals will start trusting you as soon as you show them that you value their lifestyle and you're willing to adjust yours so as to fit into their society. On the contrary, you can be completely isolated if you try to force your own values and beliefs into the local community.

When trying to blend in with the local community, it is of utmost importance that you learn the local language so as to avoid language barrier. Learning the local language will also help you save the money that could have been used in hiring a translator.

- Considering religion when interacting with the locals

In countries that embrace radical Islamism or 'Sharia Laws', women are prohibited from talking to strangers or even walking on the streets unaccompanied by their husbands or a male relative. It is also illegal for a woman to drive in countries such as Saudi Arabia. This means that you must be very careful when visiting such countries so as not to fall on the wrong side of the law. Keep in mind that the penalty for breaking these laws is being stoned to death in public.

- Positive personal attributes

So as to nurture good personal relationship with the local community in a foreign country, you must always be friendly, understanding and social. Nobody wants to be friends or be associated with a rude sociopath who is always quarreling with other people.

How to Invest While Abroad

After moving to a foreign country to work or do business, the next thing that comes in mind is how and where you're going to invest your savings. Some people prefer investing back home while others prefer investing in the new country. Either way, you still have to consider the many advantages and disadvantages of investing in a foreign country or back home.

Investing back home while still working/living abroad could prove to be quite difficult as you'll not be there physically to ensure that you get value for your money. However, you can still invest in the stock market as it will be quite easy to follow the paper trail. One major advantage of investing in the stock market is that you don't need to be physically present because your stock broker can do everything on your behalf. You can also dispose off your shares in a given company whenever you want.

You can also invest your money in other types of businesses such as the real estate or hospitality industry as long as you have somebody you can entrust to do the investment on your behalf. If you opt to invest your money this way, you might be forced to come back home frequently just to make sure that everything is going smoothly and that your money is not being wasted. Depositing your money in a bank account that accrues interest is also one of the ways in which you can save your money while abroad. The main advantage of this type of investment is that there is no risk at all. You can also rest assured that your money is not being swindled in any way. However, the rate at which the interest accrues is slightly lower than the rate at which real property and other businesses appreciate.

If you're thinking of investing in a foreign country, you have to consider how secure your money will be. You also have to consider how locals perceive foreigners in their country. There was a time between late 2007 and early 2008 when all foreigners owning businesses in some parts of South Africa were chased away and their businesses looted. Before investing your hard earned money abroad, it's always important that you make sure that the local citizens are not xenophobic (the fear of foreign nationals) in any way.

It is also important that you consider local laws before registering a company or opening branches in foreign countries. In most countries, international companies or businesses owned by foreign nationals must cede a given percentage shareholding to the locals. This means that you probably have to avoid such countries if you are one of those people who prefer owning 100% shares in your company.

Seeking dual citizenship is one of the ways in which you can invest in a foreign country without having to be treated like a foreigner. If the local laws allow dual citizenship and you qualify to be a citizen, then there is no reason as to why you cannot invest there if you have a deep desire to do so.

Local government policy is also one of the things that you have to consider before investing abroad. Whereas most countries encourage foreign investments, some governments deliberately place hurdles that make it quite difficult for foreigners to own businesses. Before making up your mind about investing away from home, you have to carefully analyze how the government is handling this issue. You can consult other expats with investments there so as to establish their experiences.

When thinking of investing in a foreign country, it is always important that you establish whether there are any bilateral agreements between your home country and the local government. You can save a lot of money and make huge profits by simply taking advantage of bilateral agreements between two governments. For example, you can be exempted from import or export duty if the agreement stipulates so.

What You Must Never Do in a Foreign Land

After settling in another country, you must always be extra careful so as not to get in any trouble. There are several things, places, businesses or even people that you should avoid if you want to stay in a foreign country without experiencing many problems. If you find yourself in the wrong place at the wrong time, doing the wrong thing with the wrong people, you can end up in jail, deported, heartbroken, crippled or even dead. Here are some of the things that you must try to avoid as much as possible when not in your home country.

- Engaging or doing business with criminals

Even if you're not abroad you still have to make sure that you never do any business with criminals such as drug and human traffickers, illegal gangs and cartels, money launderers, extortionists or thieves. A wise man once said that what looks like a dog, barks like a dog, smells like a dog, behaves like a dog and walks with dogs is definitely a dog. You can easily be mistaken for a criminal if you like hanging out with criminals in a foreign country.

Apart from avoiding criminals, you have to make sure that you are not engaging in any unlawful activities while there. Unlike the locals who will be freed after serving their sentence, you will be deported after serving the same sentence as the locals. By engaging in criminal activities, you can also be blacklisted on international criminals list and hence be the subject of discrimination whenever you visit other countries.

- Corporate espionage

The fact that corporate espionage is an illegal activity should be enough reason to stop you from engaging in it while abroad. Large, international companies highly value their secrets and hence they can do anything as long as their secrets remain secret. This means that you can easily be harmed or jailed for years if you're ever caught engaging in corporate espionage while in another country.

- Getting too emotionally attached

Even if you're so comfortable in another country, you still have to make sure that you don't fall in love with the country or get emotionally attached with it unless you are planning to spend the rest of your life there. You'll find yourself depressed and missing that country once you move back home. Instead of doing something else it's very important that you strive hard towards achieving your goals in that country. However, you should note that this doesn't mean that you should not engage with the locals or that you should not like anything.

- Caution when acquiring property or doing business

In some countries such as Singapore, there is a limit to the maximum size and/or location of land that a foreigner can own. Before you acquire any property, it is important that you consult local lawyers to advice you on the maximum size and location of real property that you can acquire. In other countries, hefty taxes are imposed on foreigners and hence it will be illogical to acquire properties in such countries. Before you decide to acquire an apartment or condo, it's important that you analyze the average resell price so as to establish whether you need to buy it or simply rent one.

So as to reduce unemployment rates, most countries bar foreigners from engaging in certain businesses including retailing, hawking, cultivation and any other business that requires unskilled labor. If you're caught engaging in such businesses, you'll probably end up being imprisoned for several months before being deported to your home country. It is therefore important that you seek advice from local lawyers before making up your mind to start any business.

- Visiting insecure areas/regions

The most important thing when moving into a foreign country is not getting money or enjoying yourself but coming back home safe and sound. You must always ensure that you're totally safe regardless of what you're doing there. This means that you must try as much as possible to avoid areas experiencing sporadic violence or those with high violent crime rates. Bear in mind that even countries with the lowest crime rates still experience some criminal activities even though it is rare. You should also try to avoid being at certain places during odd hours or being caught between rival groups/factions.

- Driving without or with an invalid license

The fact that you have a driving license back home doesn't mean that you can drive a car in a foreign country. Most countries insist that foreigners must enroll in local driving schools before they can be issued with a driving license. At these schools, you're expected to learn about all the rules and laws that must be followed by motorists.

- Working without permit

One of the easiest ways to land behind bars is working in a foreign country without or with an expired work permit. Government officials might feel like you despise them or you have total disregard for the law. They'll therefore do everything they can to make sure that you're jailed for as long as the law permits.

- Running unregistered business or organizations

When in another country (applies also back home) you must never run an unregistered organization or business even if it's for charity, non-profit or you're simply volunteering. This rule mostly applies in those countries with political instability as some local political leaders might think that you're trying to finance their opponents or worse still dislodge them from power.

- Continue staying on an expired visa

Globally, it is illegal to continue staying in any country on an expired visa. Even if there are loopholes or weaknesses in government institutions, remember that you will still be jailed if you're ever caught breaking this law. If it's necessary that you extend your stay there, you can renew your visa and extend the expiration day by a few more weeks. It is also important that you stick to what brought you to that country. If for example you enter a given country on a tourist visa and then start doing some charity activities or business you'll probably be arrested and deported or even jailed.

- Students must never work for more than the maximum permissible hours per week

In spite of the fact that foreign students are allowed to work in countries such as the United Kingdom, there is a limit to the maximum number of hours that they are allowed to work each week. This piece of legislation is meant to make sure that foreign students achieve their main objective while there. If you're caught exceeding the maximal permissible hours, you can be banned from working while studying there or your student visa can be cancelled.

- Avoid being isolated

Can you imagine of what is going to happen if you need emergency medical assistance or maybe you're being attacked or your house is on fire? Unless you have good interpersonal relationships with your neighbors, nobody will be there to provide help when you need it most. It is therefore important that you interact with your neighbors and avoid living an isolated lifestyle.

Conclusion

Now you have everything you need to move into a foreign country and comfortably stay there for as long as you want. However, you should be prepared to face several challenges during the first few weeks or months after moving there. In any case, you're neither the first nor the last person to live away from your home country. You can therefore rest assured that you will soon adjust to life in a foreign country just like the way other expats adapted.

Immediately after settling in the new country, it's important that you establish contact with other expats especially those from your home country. You must also register or get the contact details of your country's foreign mission there. These are the people who will help you if you're having problems or in case you're arrested.

After staying abroad for some time, it's important that your evaluate yourself so as to know whether you've achieved your objectives or you're on your way to achieving them. If you haven't achieved anything, you probably need to do something about it by moving back home or changing your lifestyle. If you're a student with financial problems and your current salary is not helping much, you can try switching to another job and see if things will change. Those working for international organizations such as the UN can request a transfer back to their home countries or to other foreign countries if they are not comfortable with the current working conditions.

The most important thing when doing business or working abroad is to be able to note when something is amiss or not going as planned. This way you can be able to promptly adjust your lifestyle or business strategy.

By simply implementing the ideas listed in this book, you're guaranteed of coming back home much happier and/or richer than you left.

Author Bio

Colvin Tonya Nyakundi

Colvin Tonya Nyakundi is a professional freelance writer and co-author of 'How to Prepare and Survive in a Foreign Country.' Apart from that book, he has a portfolio of several other publications accumulated in the more than two years that he has been freelancing through www.odesk.com.

In addition to his interest in survival books he has authored several personal relationship, travel and holiday guides, and real estate publications. Other books that he has co-authored include 'How to Improve Your Communication Skills,' 'Construction Guide for New Investors in Real Estate,' 'How to Identify the Perfect Holiday Destination' and How to Transform a Small Business into a Multimillion Dollar Enterprise.' You can get in touch with him through his official Facebook account, tonyanc@facebook.com.

Check out some of the other JD-Biz Publishing books

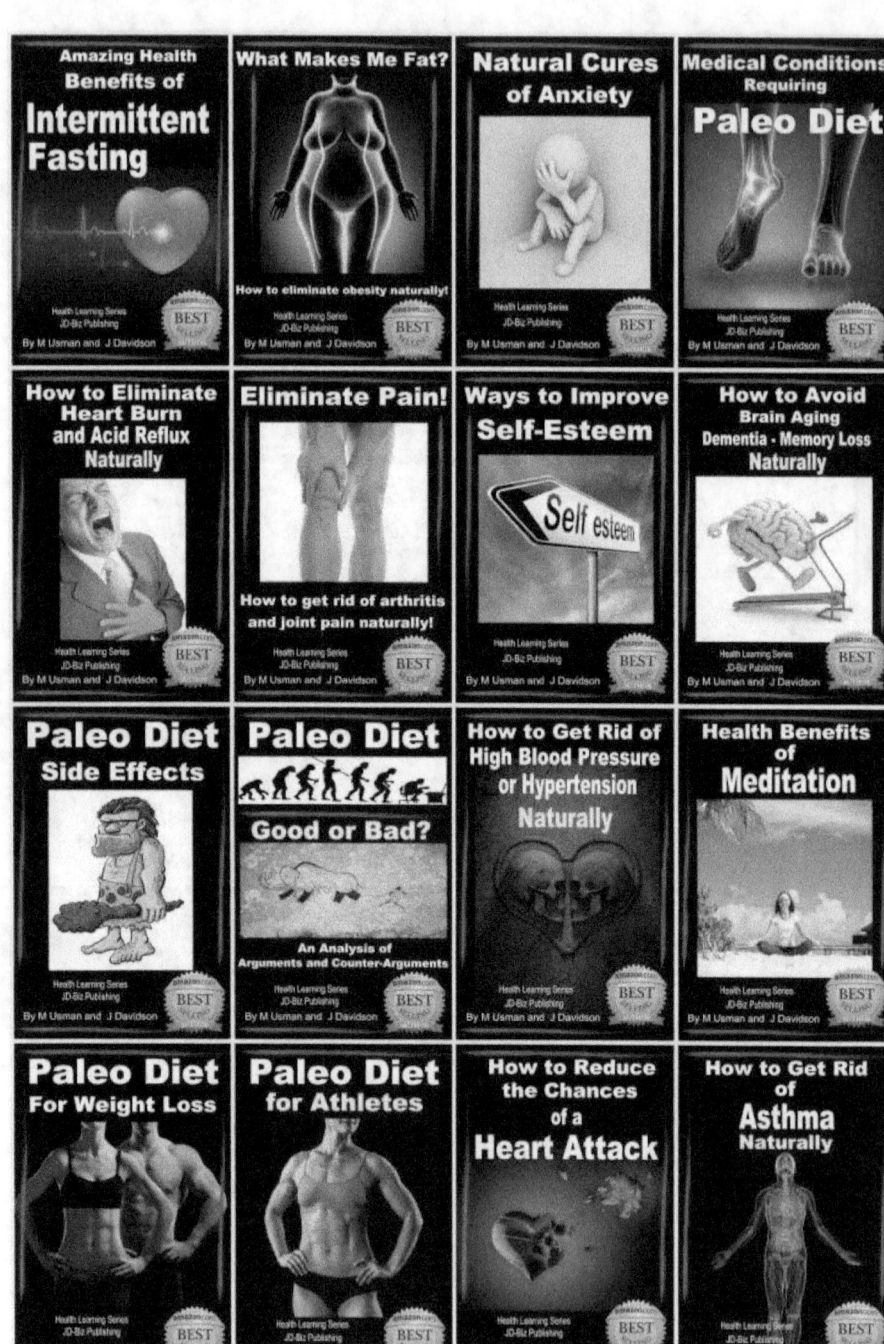

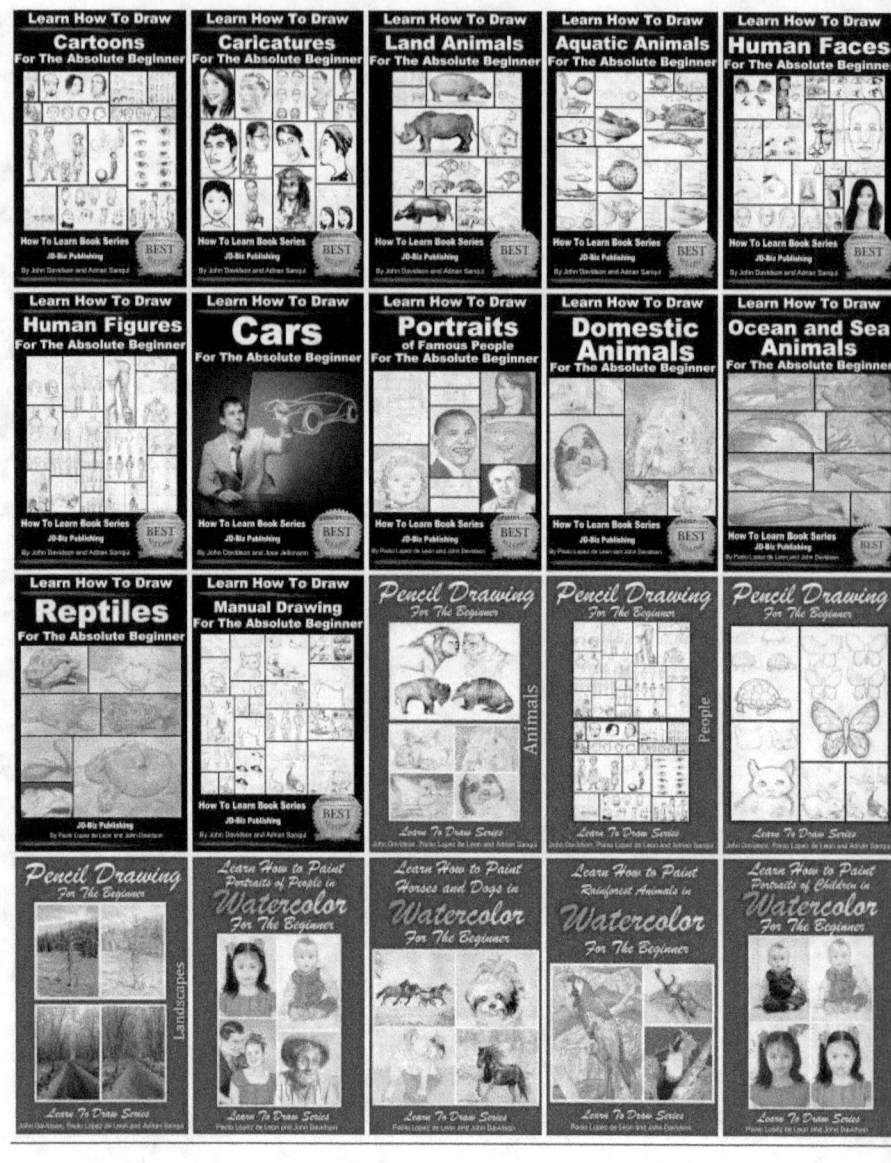

Our books are available at

1. Amazon.com

2. Barnes and Noble

3. Itunes

4. Kobo

5. Smashwords

6. Google Play Books

Publisher

JD-Biz Corp

P O Box 374

Mendon, Utah 84325

http://www.jd-biz.com/

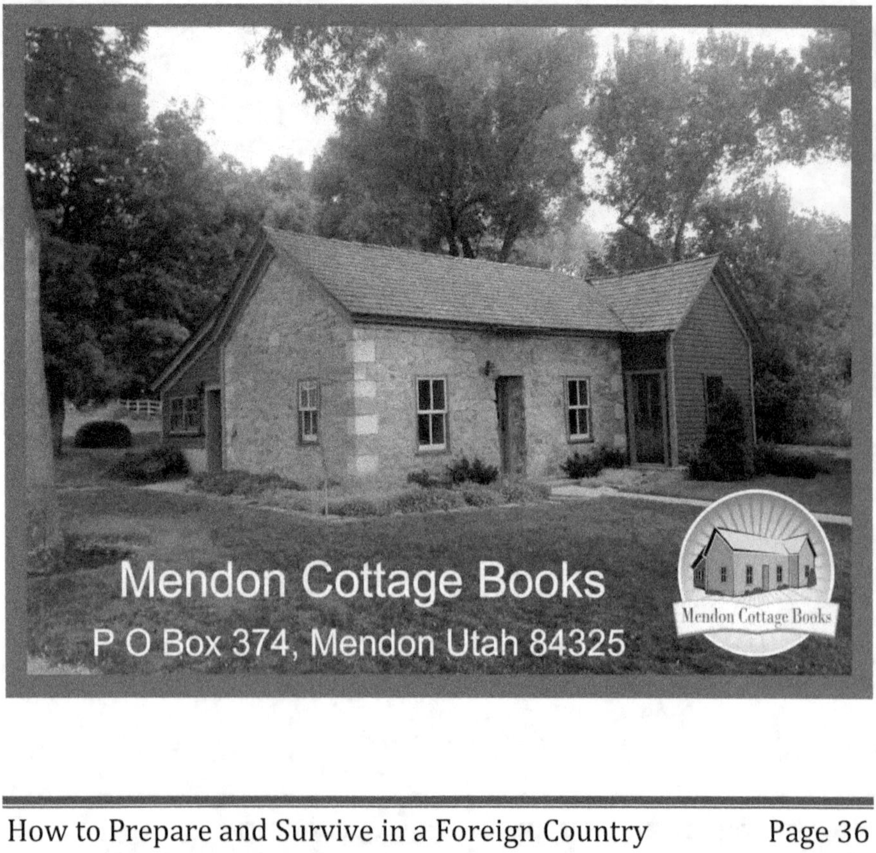

Mendon Cottage Books

P O Box 374, Mendon Utah 84325

Mendon Cottage Books